This edition first published in 2003 by

Chrysalis Children's Books
An imprint of Chrysalis Books Group
The Chrysalis Building, Bramley Road,
London W10 6SP

Consultant: Michael Chinery

British Library Cataloguing in Publication Data is available from the British Library.

ISBN 184138 922 6

Printed in China

I am a Frog

Written By
Linda Bygrave

Illustrated by
Louise Voce

Chrysalis Children's Books

I am a frog.
When I sit down ...
I look like this.

When I leap into the air ...
I look like this.

I am green and slimy
and I have to live near water -
usually ponds and streams.

I am a great swimmer because
my feet are webbed. That means
I have skin between my toes.

My long back legs are strong.
I can jump really high!
I have five toes on each of my back feet ...

but only four toes on each front foot.
I don't have a tail, but I did when
I was a baby.

I have big eyes on the top
of my head.
I don't have eyelids like you.

But when I am swimming,
a special skin covers my eyes
to keep out the water.

On land, I breathe the same way you do. I use my lungs to breathe air in and out.

But I can do something you can't.
I can breathe underwater.
I breathe through my slimy skin.

I like to eat small slugs and snails.
If I can't find those, I eat
caterpillars and woodlice.

Sometimes I like to catch
a nice, fat, juicy worm.

I gulp at insects
that come too close
to my mouth.

I have a great, big, wide mouth,
but no teeth. So I just swallow
my food whole. Yum-yum!

I have my babies in the spring.
Lots of us gather together and
at night the mummy frogs lay eggs.

Each mummy frog lays about two
thousand eggs covered in a clear jelly.
This jelly makes the eggs float.

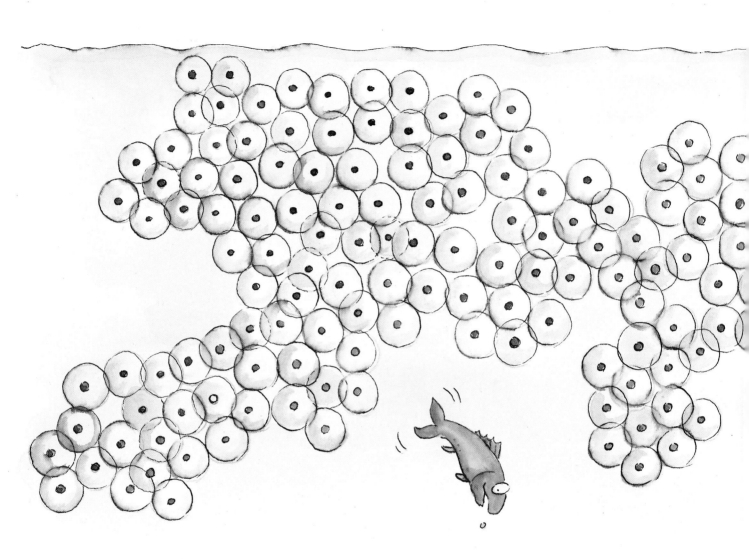

The eggs in the jelly are called
frogspawn. There is lots
and lots of it in ponds in spring.

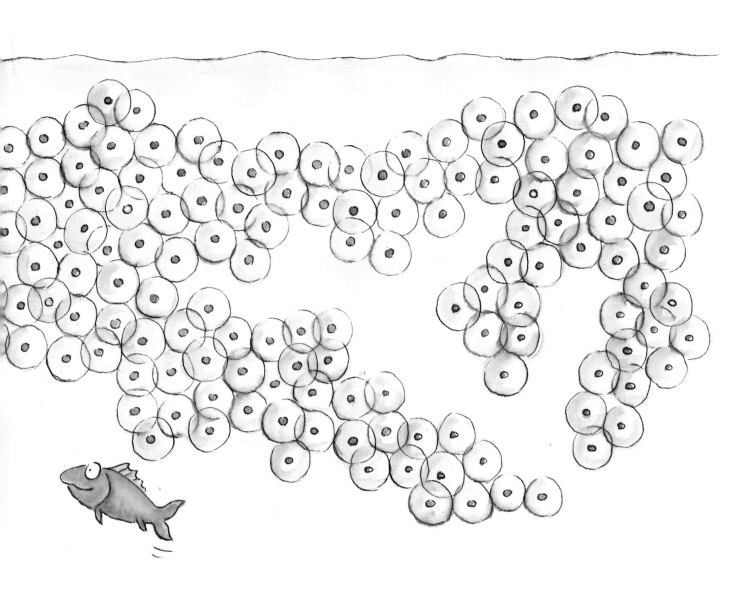

The jelly protects the eggs
from enemies and the cold.
It breaks apart after about two weeks.

The eggs turn into tiny tadpoles.
That is the name for baby frogs.
The tadpoles wriggle out of the jelly.

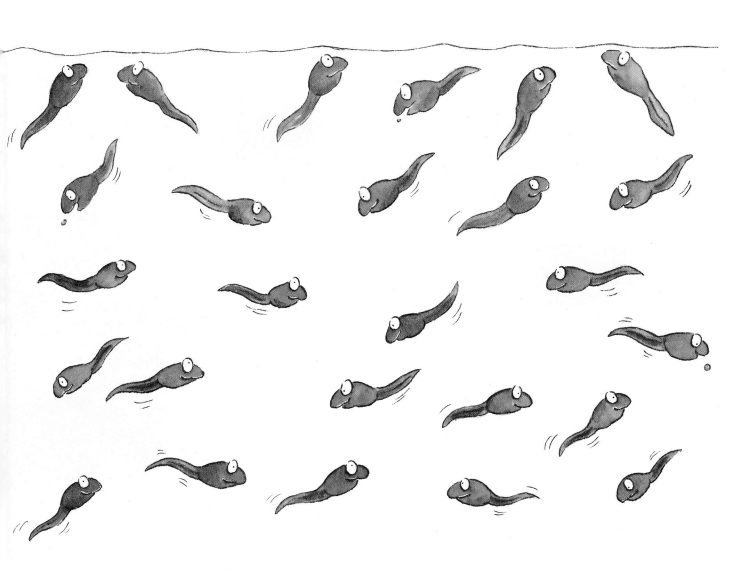

They don't look like grown-up frogs,
do they? They are small, very dark
and have tails.

After about eight weeks
the tadpoles grow back legs.
They still have a very long tail.

When they are three months old
little front legs appear. And look ...
their tails have become much shorter.

Soon they have wide mouths just like me.
But they are only froglets.
They won't be as big as me for ages.

When they are about three years old, perhaps they will have babies of their own. I'm off for a swim. Goodbye!